DEDICATION

This book it dedicated to Mom (aka Ma) for making me slow down and enjoy my surroundings.

To my clients that showed me how much infor¬mation was needed to be shared. I kept you in mind as I progressed in the writing of this book.

Other Books with Gladys as an author or Contributing Author

101 Create Ways to Attract and Retain Quality Staff by Gladys Monroy Boutwell available on Amazon.com

The Gratitude Project: Celebrating 365 Days of Gratitude 2013 Edition by Donna Kozik available on Amazon.com

Heart of a Toastmaster by Sheryl L. Roush available at SparklePresentations.com Author

HEALTH
INSURANCE
SECRETS REVEALED

GLADYS MONTROY BOUTWELL

Quantity sales and special discounts are available on quantity purchases by corporations, associations, and others. For details, contact the publisher at the address above.

Orders by U.S. trade bookstores and wholesalers. Email info@ BeyondPublishing.net

The Beyond Publishing Speakers Bureau can bring authors to your live event. For more information or to book an event contact the Beyond Publishing Speakers Bureau speak@BeyondPublishing.net

The Author can be reached directly at BeyondPublishing.net

Manufactured and printed in the United States of America distributed globally by BeyondPublishing.net

BEYOND
PUBLISHING

New York | Los Angeles | London | Sydney

ISBN Softcover: 978-1-63792-658-1
ISBN Hardcover: 978-1-63792-657-4

DISCLAIMER

This purpose of the book is to educate and entertain. The author or publisher does not guarantee that anyone following the techniques, suggestions, tips, ideas, or strategies will become successful. The author and publisher shall have neither liability nor responsibility to anyone with respect to any loss or damage caused, or alleged to be caused, directly or indirectly by the information contained in this book.

"*Gladys spends the time to hear the needs of her clients and then lays out options for you to choose from in a very easy, digestible language. No longer leaving me (or you) to spend the time investigating or translating insurance language to make sure you end up with the right plan.*"

Dr. Emalee Knudsen – Oregon

"*Even as a health care professional, health insurance plans always confused me. But after learning Gladys' secrets, tips, and simple questions to ask myself before choosing a plan, I am confident I can choose a plan that best fits my family's needs!*"

Willow Cook, Pharm.D. – Oregon

"*Gladys is the most "get it done" person I have ever met! She has so many options for employee benefits and health insurance it boggles the mind! I can't recommend her highly enough!*"

Dr. Louise Debreczeny, INSL Institute – Washington

"*As someone at age 9 whose family was significantly impacted by our nation's complex health care system when my father was diagnosed with Multiple Sclerosis, I am an ardent supporter of Gladys' book. Health care can be very complicated and difficult to understand, especially when you are not feeling well and are under a lot of stress. Gladys makes the process easier by sharing proactive ideas and tips to help educate us on how to get the right plan, at the right time, and the right price. As a trusted advisor, she "rides shotgun" through the process to ensure optimal choices are made.*

Congratulations to Gladys for her stewardship in writing this extremely valuable book. I know everyone that takes the time to read it will benefit."

Sue Lehrer, Ph.D., M.S.W. – Houston, Texas

HEALTH
INSURANCE
SECRETS REVEALED

How to understand health insurance and choose the right plan for you and your family. Even, if you are on an employer sponsored plan.

- Quick and easy tips to translate insurance language
- Confidently choose an agent
- Find the plan that you will love and, most importantly, one you will use

GLADYS MONTROY BOUTWELL

TABLE OF CONTENTS

Understand what it means

ACKNOWLEDGEMENTS

I thank Northwest Family Services in Milwaukie, Oregon for their partnership and support. Nothing like having a non-profit that embraced me as an individual and a supporter of the community. Your willingness to embrace me as your own only made it easier for me to serve the community.

I thank Marvin Revoal for the support as a health insurance broker. Your insight was invaluable in being able to educate America.

Thanks, Aflac, for introducing me to the insurance world, which was a path to the overall industry, and ultimately moved me into being part of a brokerage firm.

Thank you, Cathey Armillas, author of *The 9 ½ Laws of Marketing, How to Get Your Customers to Love You*, for your feedback on my first unpublished book and for helping me see that I had a lot more to offer.

Thank you Familias en Acción for humbling me with the *Madrina de Salud* award that reminded me about the importance of health equity among the Latino Community.

INTRODUCTION

Health Insurance Secrets Revealed, how to understand health insurance and choose the right plan for you and your family, even if you are on an employer sponsored plan is jam-packed with information to understand health insurance and know what you are purchasing. There is nothing worse than purchasing something only to find out that it is not what you wanted or needed and to make it worse, you cannot change without having a penalty assessed.

With the changes in the law regarding the Affordable Care Act, many people feel that they are being forced into the purchase of health insurance, while not being properly educated on what they are getting. Many simply pick the cheapest plan, only to find out that their doctor does not take their insurance or that they have to pay "everything" out of pocket. Additionally, they have nobody to answer questions or guide them to a better understanding.

It is interesting that many people who have insurance through their employer still do not understand what they have in terms of their health insurance.

- They may not realize the doctor they have seen for years is not part of the network their employer has chosen for them.
- They may not know the questions to ask when being referred to a specialist.
- They may not know to ask questions about the hospital or facility

they are being referred to so that they do not incur higher costs than necessary.

Most people do not realize that doctors and providers are there for the health of their patient and they do not necessarily know or care about the individual's network or budget concerns. They simply want to make the person feel better. Unfortunately, once they have done their part, the patient will receive a bill a month later that may cause some shock.

Knowing your medical plan, what it covers, who it covers, and how you can make the most of what you have is key in making a sound decision regarding the plan that you choose and if it is worth the price that you will pay now or later.

Having been in corporate America for 20 years, now an insurance producer, and having helped over 1000 families with their insurance needs, I know the questions and concerns that every family asks every time. This is a quick read that will provide you with top quality advice on picking your plan and knowing how to use it.

1

I DON'T KNOW ANYTHING ABOUT INSURANCE

DON'T BE AFRAID OF LACK
OF UNDERSTANDING

Over 500 conversations over a period of six months started with, *"Before we start, I want you to know that I don't know anything about insurance. Even when I had it with my last company, I never knew exactly what I had or if I had a good plan. . ."*

You are probably having the same feeling right about now, right?

Nothing like buying something that you know you need (or that you feel you are being forced to get), but you don't know what to do with it or how to use it.

This book acts as your guide to understanding your health insurance, what you are getting, how to choose what to get, how to find the right person to help you, and how to use it once you have it.

If you have never had insurance, this book clarifies what you should get or already have.

Even if you have a plan with your employer, you will find answers to the many questions that were not answered when you got that stack of papers to fill out to get your plan.

After all, don't you just want to understand what you are buying, and have it work for you?

Let's have some fun!

WHY DO I NEED HEALTH INSURANCE?

"Obama said that I need to get health insurance," said Juana as she sat next to me.

You may laugh at this statement; however, it was said many times. A large majority of people looking into health insurance feel a sense of being pushed into getting health insurance because of the Affordable Care Act.

Although this may be a true statement, The Consumers Health Insurance Authority (HealthInsurance.info) stated that there are a variety of reasons why people purchase health insurance. Forbes gave ten reasons why people get health insurance:

1. May protect you from the risk of uncertain bills for health care. May pay for services that you use often.
2. Without it, you may not be able to afford certain (expensive) services.
3. May pay for services that you use often.
4. May help you to get better quality care as a member of a coordinated health plan than you would get on your own.
5. May not need to worry about the cost of care when you are sick.
6. The additional money paid by your insurance carrier when you are sick may be more valuable to you than money when you are well.
7. You may get more out of a family policy if your family consists of more than two people.
8. You may get more from your policy than most people if you or your dependents have more health care needs than most people.
9. If you are on an employer plan, you may not pay income tax on your benefits; therefore, it is more valuable per dollar than the same amount in taxable pay.
10. Health insurance companies generally pay lower prices to doctors and hospitals than you would pay on your own.

You do not need to go-at-it alone. You can search for help and get it for free.

You can search for a local health insurance agent or broker at the National Association of Health Underwriter's website. An agent can help you find and guide you through what can be a complicated application process. Be sure that the agent has experience with health insurance (not just life, disability, or your home/auto). Feel free to ask if they get compensated for selling certain plans or policies. A good sign that they're working in your best interest is if they ask about your eligibility for COBRA, spouse's plan, and/or government programs.

UNDERSTANDING WHAT HEALTH INSURANCE IS

Julie walks into the office for our first meeting. She looks perplexed and rattles off a slew of questions all at once, *"Does my insurance include dental? How many times can I visit my doctor? Can I visit my current doctor? Do I have to pay to see my doctor? The last time, I got a bill after having blood drawn, why? Frankly Gladys, I just don't get it. How can you help me?"*

Like Julie, if you are reading this book, it is because you want to not only know how to choose a plan, but also understand what health insurance is.

Some of these questions that Julie posed are questions that you, too, may have:

- What am I paying for?
- What are my monthly costs?

- Why are my doctor's visits not free?
- Can I see my current doctor?
- Why do I still need to pay for my laboratories or x-rays?
- What is the difference between all the plans and all the insurance companies?

Health insurance is a contract between you and the health insurance company. Like any contract, it states that you pay a portion of the medical expenses, and the insurance company pays a portion of your medical expenses.

With the Affordable Care Act, it now specifies that insurance companies will pay medical expenses related to preventing you from getting sick. What does this mean? It means that you do not have to pay for most preventive services, such as yearly check-ups, mammograms, prostate exams, and immunizations (to name a few).

The contract states what coverage you have and defines what the insurance company will pay. This includes how much you must pay (co-pay and deductible) to see the doctor or specialist and the amount that you must pay before the insurance covers a certain percentage (co-insurance).

UNDERSTANDING WHAT HEALTH INSURANCE IS NOT

"What do you mean that I have to pay? I thought that Obama said that I would get free insurance," said Mario.

First, Health Insurance is not free. The changes in the law and the Affordable Care Act do not provide free insurance to all residents, nor does it mean that services will be free once you pay your monthly premium.

Second, you pay monthly premiums to have health insurance, just in case something happens. This means that you will need to continue to pay for your insurance every month, even if you do not see the doctor or get sick. Health insurance is like your automobile insurance, it is a good thing if you do not need to use it and it is a great thing if you do.

Third, insurance companies want to collect your money and not have to pay out claims. This is no surprise as they are in the business of making money and are not providing insurance for their health (no pun intended). Even not-for-profit carriers want to make money in order to re-invest in their plans or offerings.

DO NOT UNDERESTIMATE WHAT YOU ALREADY KNOW

You need to select the plan that best fits your needs this coming year and that will allow you to balance needs with costs. After all, you can make changes to your plan and your carrier every year during Open Enrollment. You may know more about your insurance than you think.

- You may know what doctor, provider, or hospital you may want to have included in your insurance plan.
- You may also know what services you may want or need.
- You may also know if you may need an expensive procedure to be performed.

This is all great information to know when picking your plan, which we will review in a later chapter.

For now, you need to know where you are in your current

knowledge. To find that out, here are a few Pre-Test questions to get you started:

1. What is a deductible?
   a) What you do before you get hit by a ball
   b) The amount you pay before your insurance kicks in
   c) The amount you take away from the total bill
2. What is the difference between co-pay and coinsurance?
   a) Co-pay and co-insurance are the amount paid by a co-worker
   b) Co-pay is a set dollar amount and coinsurance is a percent
   c) Co-pay is a percent and co-insurance is a set amount
3. What is an open enrollment period?
   a) The time period that you have to enroll in school during the summer
   b) The time period that you have to enroll or dis-enroll from an insurance plan
   c) The time period to pick a plan
4. What is the difference between the ACA (Affordable Care Act) and Obamacare?
   a) The ACA is better than Obamacare
   b) They are the exact same thing
   c) ACA is affordable, and Obamacare was created by President Obama
5. What is the difference between a PPO and an EPO?
   a) PPO is a Preferred Provider Organization that has a contract and that you do not need a referral. EPO is an Exclusive Provider Organization that exclusively provides services, referrals are needed, and the carrier will not pay if you do not use those exclusive providers.

b) PPO is better than an EPO

c) EPO is better than a PPO

6. What is a Network?

   a) The people that you hang out with

   b) What the IT Department deals with on a daily basis

   c) The list of doctors, hospitals, and providers that give you the most bang-for-your-buck when getting treated for health-related services

7. What is the difference between In-Network and Out-of-Network?

   a) In-Network are doctors, hospitals, and providers that give you the most bang-for-your-buck when seeking medical treatments. Out-of-Network costs you more out-of-pocket because the doctors, hospitals, and provides do not have a contract with the insurance company

   b) In-Network are people you know, and Out-of-Network are people you do not know

   c) In-Network are system that are working, and Out-of-Network are systems that are not working, hence out-of-network

8. What is a Max Out-of-Pocket?

   a) The amount that your children take from your pocket when you have nothing else to give

   b) The maximum amount that you can afford to pay

   c) The maximum amount that you will pay for all medical services

9. Should an Agent charge me for helping me?

   a) S/he better not

   b) Yes

   c) Maybe

10. What is a qualifying event?
    a) When there is a change in status (get married, get divorced, adopt, lose a dependent, lose employer sponsored health insurance, move to a new state, change in residential status) outside of the national Open Enrollment period
    b) What allows you to go to the semi-finals of your favorite sport
    c) When your favorite sports team makes it to the next level towards a championship
11. When do I need a qualifying event for the purposes of health insurance?
    a) When something specific happens outside open enrollment period that gives you the opportunity to purchase a new health insurance plan
    b) Any time of year
    c) Only when I get sick
12. Can I be denied services for a pre-existing condition?
    a) I better not be
    b) Yes
    c) Maybe

ANSWER KEY

1. b – The amount you pay before your insurance kicks in
2. b – Co-pay is a set dollar amount and co-insurance is a percent
3. b – The time period that you have to enroll or dis-enroll from an insurance plan

4.   b – They are the exact same thing
5.   a – PPO is a Preferred Provider Organization that has a contract and that you do not need a referral. EPO is an Exclusive Provider Organization that exclusively provides services, referrals are needed, and the carrier will not pay if you do not use those exclusive providers.
6.   c – The list of doctors, hospitals, and providers that give you the most bang-for-your-buck when getting treated for health-related services
7.   a – In-Network are doctors, hospitals, and providers that give you the most bang-for-your-buck when seeking medical treatments. Out-of- Network costs you more out-of-pocket because the doctors, hospitals, and provides do not have a contract with the insurance company
8.   c – The maximum amount that you will pay for all medical services
9.   a – S/he better not
10. a – When there is a change in status (get married, get divorced, adopt, lose a dependent, lose employer sponsored health insurance, move to a new state, change in residential status) outside of the national Open Enrollment period
11. a – When something specific happens outside open enrollment period that gives you the opportunity to purchase a new health insurance plan
12. a – I better not be

2

HOW DOES THE AFFORDABLE CARE ACT AFFECT ME?

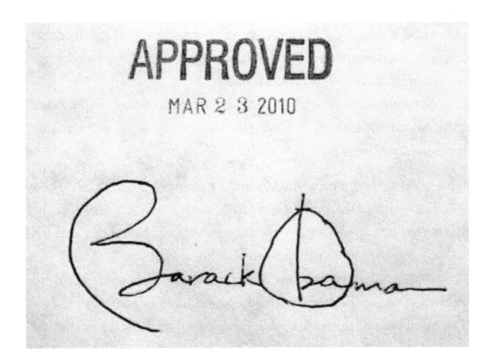

UNDERSTAND THE AFFORDABLE CARE ACT IN 3 EASY STEPS

Jimmy Kimmel serves as host and executive producer of Emmy nominated *Jimmy Kimmel Live*, ABC's late-night talk show. He is well known for huge viral video successes with 1.5 billion views on YouTube alone.

An episode that aired on October 1, 2013, entitled "Six of One – Obamacare vs. The Affordable Care Act" asked pedestrians on Hollywood Boulevard if they preferred Obamacare or The Affordable Care Act. Most supported The Affordable Care Act over Obamacare.

Hmmm… Which do you support?

As Jimmy Kimmel said, "*Which do you think is* better - Obamacare or the Affordable Care Act? *They're the same thing, but that didn't stop people from weighing in...*"

Step 1 – know the name of the law and its purpose

Know that Obamacare, The Affordable Care Act (ACA), The Patient Protection and Affordable Care Act (PPACA) are one and the same. This is the health care reform law that was passed in 2010.

The purpose of the law is to allow more people to afford healthcare, reduce healthcare spending, and have an added tax law.

You may not agree with what is happening or how it has affected you, but it is still a law. And a tax law at that. It is about who gets insurance, how much they must pay, and what it covers.

Step 2 – know what is required of you

Know that the ACA is a Tax Law. Although Section 1555 of the law allows you the freedom <u>not</u> to participate in Federal health insurance programs [Provides that no individual, company, business, nonprofit entity, or health insurance issuer shall be required to participate in any Federal health insurance program created under this Act], if you choose not to have health insurance, you may put yourself at-risk for having healthcare expenses.

There was a penalty that was 2% of adjusted gross income. However, that penalty has been reduced to 0%. Many think that the penalty was removed, but it was simply reduced to zero and it can be brought back.

It is important to shop around to find out what you may be entitled in the form of assistance before you decide if you will enroll in a plan or not.

Step 3 – know the benefits of the law

The law was designed to help ensure that you have access to effective health care coverage and to limit your out-of-pocket costs.

The law does not provide or guarantees free health insurance. There are aspects that may allow recipients to obtain free health insurance through Medicaid (state) or tax credit assistance (federal) based on income, size of household, and residency status.

Highlights of the law that may be the most pertinent to you:

- An insurance company cannot deny you coverage due to a pre-existing condition
- Annual and lifetime maximums have been eliminated
- Your child can remain on your plan until the age of 26
- Plans must maintain ten minimum essential coverage:
    1. Ambulatory patient services, such as doctor visits
    2. Hospitalization

3. Mental health and substance use disorder services, including behavioral health treatment
4. Rehabilitative and habilitative services and devices
5. Laboratory services
6. Emergency services
7. Maternity and newborn care
8. Prescription drugs
9. Preventive and wellness services and chronic disease management
10. Pediatric Services (pediatric oral care may be included or offered as part of a stand-alone plan)

- Healthcare.gov was created to help Americans understand the law
- You cannot be charged more due to health condition, gender, immigration status, or salary
- Premiums can only be based on: age, geographic area, and tobacco use
- Assistance via tax credit to use towards monthly premium costs
- Assistance via cost-sharing reducing out-of-pocket costs
- Eliminates excessive waiting periods (>90 days)
- Premiums are the same within the purchasing exchange or directly through an insurance carrier

Note: this is based before any tax credits are issued

- Allows an employer to reimburse an employee for the individual health insurance.

Done through an individual coverage health reimbursement arrangement (ICHRA). Or, if the employer has <50 employees, they can also offer a Qualified Small Employer Health Reimbursement Arrangement (QSEHRA)

Note: this reimbursement arrangement reduces the potential tax credit that the individual may possibly receive through the exchange. The individual can choose to not participate in the ICHRA and be eligible for the tax credit.

- Freedom to not participate in Federal health insurance programs
- Improved access to Medicaid by allowing states to reduce the eligibility to those with income at or below 133% of the Federal Poverty Level for non-elderly, non-pregnant individuals

   Note: not all states are participating in this option, as the law simply 'allows' states to reduce the eligibility requirement, but does not require

- Special rules pertaining to American Indians and Alaska Natives
- Annual maximum for Flexible Spending Accounts (FSA) to increase each year

   Note: 2024 at $3200

- An 80/20 Medical Loss Ratio (MLR) rule to ensure that at least 80% of premium dollars paid to health insurance carrier are spent on providing healthcare

10 Essential Health Benefits

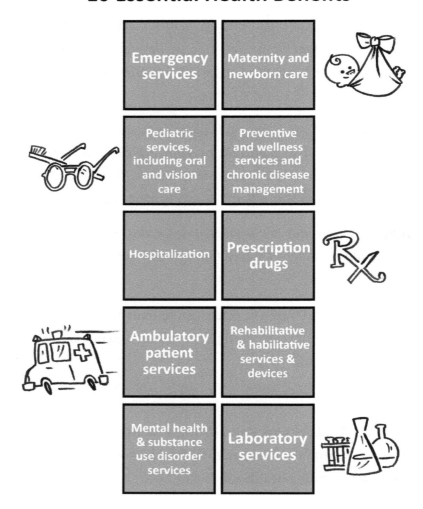

Emergency services	Maternity and newborn care
Pediatric services, including oral and vision care	Preventive and wellness services and chronic disease management
Hospitalization	Prescription drugs
Ambulatory patient services	Rehabilitative & habilitative services & devices
Mental health & substance use disorder services	Laboratory services

HOW TO BENEFIT FROM
THE AFFORDABLE CARE ACT

No matter your thoughts on the law, it is still a law. You have a choice: you can choose to participate or simply choose to incur all healthcare out-of-pocket expenses.

Before you get angry at the political aspects of it, think about the following:

- Can you obtain assistance to reduce your monthly premiums?
- Can your child(ren) benefit from being part of Medicaid or CHIP program?
- Can your out-of-pocket costs be reduced?
- Can somebody help you make this process easier?
- Can you afford to be without health coverage?
- Can you self-fund (or self-pay) for your healthcare needs?
- Can you obtain healthcare coverage through your employer?
- Can you provide healthcare coverage to yourself and your employees?

WRITE DOWN WHAT YOU NEED

"Gladys, this is my doctor, these are my 8 specialists that I go to once a month, I have 10 prescriptions filled every month, and I will need surgery in the next 6-months," said Jerry to me.

I was 'WOW' and 'I love it'. Jerry knew exactly what he needed. He did not know how to translate that to the perfect plan for him, but he knew his circumstances and what he would be facing in the coming year.

With this slew of information, I was able to research plans, reduce his out-of-pocket expenses, and find two plans that had all of his doctors within the network. This allowed Jerry to focus on his two best options for his needs rather than 20,000 plans that he did not need.

Forbes stated in an article *"It was not the insurance plan itself that cures or kills you."* They go on to state that your health insurer (the insurance company) decides what physicians to offer through their network and studies show some doctors and medical groups pay more attention to preventive medicine, disease management, and the coordination of care delivery.

You acknowledged that you may not know what you don't know, you have tested your current knowledge, and now you need to ask yourself what you need.

Take a moment… Write down what you and your family needed in the past three years:

Who is your primary care physician (PCP)? _____

How many times did you see your doctor last year?

    ☐ 1-3   ☐ 4-6   ☐ 7+

How many times do you anticipate seeing your doctor this coming year?

    ☐ 1-3   ☐ 4-6   ☐ 7+

Are there any medical circumstances that you must keep track of controlling?

    ☐ No   ☐ Yes

If 'yes' to the previous question, which ones?

☐ Anemia	☐ Blood Pressure
☐ Cholesterol	☐ Crones Disease
☐ Diabetes	☐ Fibromyalgia
☐ Kidney Disease	☐ Mental Illness
☐ Other	

Did your doctor state that you needed to see him /her more often to manage chronic illnesses?

    ☐ No   ☐ Yes

If yes, how often?

☐ 1x per month	☐ Every 2-5 months
☐ Every 6-months	

Were you referred to a specialist?

    ☐ No   ☐ Yes

If you were referred to a specialist, what kind and what is his/her name? _____

How often will I need to see him/her?

    ☐ 1x per month   ☐ Every 2-5 months

    ☐ Every 6 months

Do you have planned surgery?

    ☐ No ☐ Yes,

    If yes, when?:   For what?: _____

Who is/are your surgeon(s)? _

What is the closest hospital to you or your preferred hospital?

How much do you have saved or plan to save towards medical costs?:

Doctors	$ _____
Specialists	$ _____
Rx	$ _____
Laboratory, x-rays, imaging	$_____
Alternative medicine	$ _____
Other medical expenses	$ _____

Do you have a Flexible Spending Account (FSA) or Health Savings Account (HSA) to help with your medical costs?

    ☐ No   ☐ Yes, If yes, how much: $ _____

Would you rather pay more monthly or when you see your doctor/specialist?

☐ More Monthly   ☐ More when I see my doctor/specialist or have procedures done

Would you rather pay less monthly or have lower out-of-pocket costs for procedures, laboratories, and specialists?
☐ Less Monthly   ☐ Less when I have procedures, labs, or see a specialist

Do you prefer or need alternative medicine providers, such as chiropractor, acupuncturist, or naturopath?
☐ No   ☐ Yes

Do you take monthly medications? ☐ No   ☐ Yes

Do you currently have insurance? If so, have you used it?

☐ No   ☐ Yes

If you have not, why not? ____

If you did, did you compare your explanation of benefits with your bills?
☐ No   ☐ Yes

Were the providers that you saw within or outside of your network?
☐ No   ☐ Yes

How much did you spend in the last three years on doctors, specialists, medications, alternative medicine, and other medical needs?
$ _____

SELECTING YOUR POLICY

Whether you're trying to decide what plan to get through your employer (some offer choices) or trying to decide on an individual health plan, you need to consider your needs first.

- Do you want a plan that covers preventive care like annual check-ups?
- How healthy are you? If you need a low premium and are healthy, you might consider a plan with a higher deductible plan.

  Keep in mind that accidents happen, and a single hospital stay could wipe out your savings and put you into debt. Think about how much money you would be able to put toward medical expenses if it should become necessary.
- Do you have a specific doctor or hospital you want to be able to go to?

  Remember that managed care plans use networks of doctors, and unless your doctor is in that network, you'll pay all or some of the bills whenever you see them.
- How important is it to you to have easy access to specialists without a referral?

Many managed care plans require a referral from your primary care physician before you can see a specialist. If they don't feel it's necessary, then you'll be paying for the visit out of your own pocket.

I know you may want to know what it is all going to cost you and you want to understand what 'it' all means. We will get there. Right now, you need to clarify your needs before you move forward.

Why? Because if you are not clear about what you want or need, you will not know what to look for.

Understanding your needs clearly is key to finding a plan that will work for you. Otherwise, **you will be spending money without getting any use out of it.** It will be like buying heavy-duty machinery that looks great, you know it is useful, but you do not have a need for it. It will simply collect dust.

In more simple terms, you purchase a treadmill for hanging clothes. Not its intended purpose. You know it is a good buy and you know it will be useful. . . IF you use it. Insurance is the same; it is great IF you use it and IF you know how to use it.

Look back at the previous questions and how you answered them. The doctors, specialists, alternative care providers, medications, and all medical needs must be taken into consideration when looking at plans.

If your personal needs differ from that of other family members, you may need different coverage than they do.

- Is there anything that stood out for you?
- If so, what was it?
- Is it something that you will need to address this coming year?

Keep these things in mind as you choose a plan. Feel free to take your questions to an Agent who will use your answers to find the best fit for you and your family.

3

AGENTS AND BROKERS

GET AN AGENT/BROKER

Rock stars, actors, and artists all have agents. Why do they have agents, you ask? Without an agent, they would be lost!

The purpose of a rock star, actor, or artist agent is to find them gigs, answer questions, remove unnecessary communication, and ultimately, streamline the process.

Essentially, the same goes for your Health Insurance Agent/Broker. Their purpose is to answer your questions, help you navigate through the oceans of information, and guide you down the road that will help get you what you ultimately want, a streamlined process to picking your insurance.

Simple, isn't it?

Insurance Agents have gone through training,

testing, certification, and are hopefully, keeping up with the trends and regulations of the industry.

Your insurance agent/broker should be somebody that you can talk to, ask questions, and get answers that you can understand. Now, you may not always get the answer that you want, but the point is to have a go-to person when you are in doubt.

When you are picking your plan, have a question on your network and coverage, or need to file a claim, you should feel like the Allstate commercial, "You're in good hands."

Your agent/broker should be able to guide you through the process of finding the right plan for

you and your family and still be there months later to answer a question or help file a claim.

Have I mentioned: "They should be there for you?"

DON'T PAY YOUR AGENT/BROKER

Ouch! Sounds harsh and even brings a "Huh?" to you, right?

If you use an Agent or purchase your own insurance, you pay the same premium. The reason for this is that Agents are paid commission by the Insurance Company (Carrier) and the company has already embedded the commission within the premium.

This means that you do not need to pay the Agent, as the Carrier compensates us agents once you pay your monthly premium.

Now, that being said, some states will not allow you to use an agent if you are getting a tax subsidy. Essentially, you either forego the tax credit for the option of having somebody help you or you are on your own in picking a plan.

Harsh, isn't it?

If you are in a state that has this rule, you now have this book to help guide you in finding a plan. However, if you are in a state that does allow you to use an Agent, then, I suggest that you use an Agent.

If your state utilizes the Federally Facilitated Marketplaces (FFM), they do NOT directly appoint, compensate, nor set compensation levels for agents/brokers.

In order to be compensated for assisting somebody find a plan and enroll in a qualified health plan through the Federally Facilitated Marketplace, the agent/broker must be appointed with the carrier in accordance with state law and their set agreement.

10 IMPORTANT QUESTIONS
TO ASK AGENT/BROKER

"Gee Gladys, why hadn't anybody told me that before?"

"I didn't realize that I would have to pay everything out of pocket before my plan covered me!"

"I didn't understand what that means."

These are some of the questions and comments that I heard time and time again when somebody came to me with questions about the insurance they purchased.

Most of the time, the person asked their question, and I answered it before I even knew that they had already enrolled in a plan and before they stated the above mentioned.

If you are going to choose an Agent, it is important to have one that you will be happy to work with for years to come.

If the Agent is not one that you will want to work with, you will easily change from one to another and it will be more difficult to build a relationship.

To avoid this lack of relationship building, here are 10 important questions to ask before you choose an Agent:

1) What do you specialize in?

   This question allows you to find out if the Agent works with individuals and if they focus on health insurance.

   If the Agent's specialty is voluntary products, Medicare, property and casualty, or personal lines of insurance, you may want to consider if that is who will best guide you through finding your health insurance plan.

2) How long have you been in the health insurance industry?

This question goes along with the first question. If the Agent does not know enough about the health insurance industry, you may or may not get the best plan for you and your family.

3) Do you represent one or more insurance carriers?

The purpose of this question is to know if you will see a variety of insurance carriers and plans rather than multiple plans by the same carrier.

This is important because if another carrier has a better plan or a different network of providers, you may or may not see it.

4) What do you enjoy the most about the individual health insurance industry?

This may not seem relevant; however, it will give you insight into the Agent's motivation and if it is in-line with your needs.

5) Who will help me with finding doctors that are in my network? Or: Who will help me file a claim?

This question allows you to know if the Agent will be there for you when you need their assistance.

6) How big is your agency? Or: How many people work in your office?

This question allows you to know if the Agent works by him/herself or if there are others that they partner with.

This is an important question because if the Agent is on vacation, you will know that somebody else may be able to assist you.

7) Do you or somebody in your office assist with other types of insurance?

This question allows you to know if the Agent or Agency will be able to service more than your health insurance needs.

This may be important to you if you want to have a 'one stop shop' for all your insurance needs.

8) How do I get in touch with you?

This question allows you to know how readily accessible the Agent will be to you.

Will they provide you their cell phone number or only their office number?

9) How do you communicate with your clients?

This question allows you to know how they will communicate with you: email, mail, call, or text. And, if it is your preferred communication method.

10) I don't understand, can you explain that another way?

This is such an important question. If there is anything that does not make sense or that you do not understand, it is important for the Agent to find another way of explaining it to or painting a picture that will resonate.

Do not be afraid and ask as many questions as come to mind.

See how the Agent reacts to your questions and if they are genuinely interested in helping you or if they become frustrated.

If you ask questions, you are in control of the situation and you will know if the Agent you are speaking with is the Agent that you feel comfortable assisting you.

And, keep in mind: You can always fire your Agent if you are not happy with their performance.

Other Question to Ask

When do you pay your medical bill?

- AFTER you review your Explanation of Benefits.
- The reason for this is because your procedures may have been preventive instead of diagnostic. You may have been overcharged because they may have been incorrectly coded.

4

HOW DO I CHOOSE A PLAN?

GET A COMPARISON

"I want to know my options," was a statement made by every person with whom I spoke.

If you want to know you are getting the best deal, you need to compare.

This is similar to buying a car. You may know the brands that you would consider, you have certain amenities that you must have, and you know how much you are willing to spend.

The same goes for health insurance. You need to know the carriers, the plan details, and the cost. If you are getting more options from one carrier at a price that is slightly more to another with fewer options, you may opt to spend those dollars to get those options, if you are going to use those options.

You can comparison shop at various online sites such as ehealthinsurance.com, healthinsurance.com, or insuremonkey.com.

Note: Be aware that you may start to get unwanted emails on a lot of the comparison sites. I suggest you stay prudent and utilize your state's health insurance marketplace or healthcare.gov as your main comparison options.

Here is an example of a comparison of what the insurance will pay:

	BRONZE	SILVER	GOLD
Calendar year deductible per	$6,500	$4,250	$1,500
Calendar year deductible per family	$13,000	$8,500	$3,000
Calendar year maximum out of pocket per person	$9,450	$9,100	$7,000
Calendar year maximum out of pocket per family	$18,900	$18,200	$14,000
Primary Care (PCP)	$50 *	First 3 visits $5 *, then $45 *	$20 *
Specialist	$100 *	$65 *	$40 *
Urgent Care	$100	$65 *	$40 *
Inpatient care (including maternity)	50%	30%	20%
Outpatient x-rays & labs	50%	30%	20%
Emergency Room	50%	30%	20%
Alternative care	Not Covered	$40 *	$25 *
Generic	$20 *	$20 *	$10 *
Preferred Brand	no charge after ded	$65 *	$40 *
Non-Preferred Brand	no charge after ded	50% *	50% *
Preferred Specialty	no charge after ded	50% *	20% *
Non-Preferred Specialty	no charge after ded	50% *	50% *

Indicates the deductible is waived

	HMO	PPO	POS	HSA
Who is this plan best for?	Families interested in preventiative care or requiring ongoing care	Those that want an HMO sytle plan with more freedom of choice	Those that know how to use their plan and that can select HMO, PPO, or FFS payment methods at the time of service	Healthy individuals, careful health care users above median income levels, self-employed, and small business owners.
Flexiblity in choosing	Limited	Moderate	Moderate High	High
Deductible	Lowest to Moderate	Moderate	Moderate High	High
Monthly Premiums	Low	Moderate	Moderate High	Lowest
Copayments/ Coinsurance	Pay lower copayments for medical expenes, doctor visits, hospitalization, Rx, etc.	Pay low to medium copayments for medical expenes, doctor visits, hospitalization, Rx, etc.	Depends on method of payment plan selected at time of service.	First dollar responsibility. Usually, a health savings account is used to save and used to pay for qualified medical expenses.

Deductible

"*A what? What's a deductible?*" Does this sound familiar?

Maybe you have heard it being said, but you may not know what it means.

A deductible is the amount that you, the insured, pay BEFORE the insurance pays. That's right, you have up-front costs.

Does this make sense? No worries, the next chapter will review each section of the comparison.

UNDERSTAND PLAN COMPARISONS

Getting a comparison is great; however, you need to understand what it all means. Otherwise, it would be like picking a car without really understanding all the features and if you need them.

For example, if you have a family of seven, a Mini Cooper may be in your price range, but it will not suit the needs of your family. You may want to compare an SUV with a minivan. The same goes for health insurance. You want to compare plans that have the required services.

Let's begin. . .

High level overview of the different types of

plans that you can compare.

This is like your car insurance. You must pay your deductible before the insurance company pays any claims. If your windshield cracks and

it will cost you $400 to fix, but you have a $750

deductible, the insurance will not pay anything under the $750 that you are responsible for.

Health insurance is the same. If you know that you will have medical procedures done, you may consider picking a low deductible plan so that your maximum out-of-pocket expenses are lowered.

Keep in mind, if you pay less out-of-pocket when you obtain services, you will pay more monthly.

Here are three examples of different deductibles based on the plan level. Keep in mind that within each metal tier you may encounter different deductibles.

	BRONZE	SILVER	GOLD
Calendar year deductible per person	$6,500	$4,250	$1,500
Calendar year deductible per family	$13,000	$8,500	$3,000

It is important to know how much you will be spending up-front before your insurance covers your medical costs.

In this example

- The Bronze plan has the highest deductible of $4,250 for an individual and $8,500 for a family
- The Silver plan has a mid-range deductible of $2,500 for an individual and $5,000 for a family
- The Gold plan has the lowest deductible of $500 for an individual and $1,000 for a family

Why is this important?

You must know what you will be spending. If you go into emergency, have surgery, or are hospitalized, the deductible is the up-front or first charge that you will receive before the percent (co-insurance) of your responsibility.

Example: Emergency visit (5 hours, labs, doctor, nurse, tech, etc.):

This is only the beginning of the comparison and calculation.

CO-INSURANCE AND
MAXIMUM OUT-OF-POCKET

"What if I am hospitalized? How will I know how much I will have to pay?"

We first need to know your maximum out of pocket based on your plan. This is important because it will tell you how much you are responsible for during the year before the insurance company pays 100% of all further expenses.

The maximum out-of-pocket for in and out-of-network are different. If you are having a planned surgery in an out-of-network facility, expect to pay a lot more than if you had stayed in-network with your insurance carrier.

	BRONZE	SILVER	GOLD
Calendar year maximum out of pocket per person	$9,450	$9,100	$7,000
Calendar year maximum out of pocket per family	$18,900	$18,200	$14,000

The reason you see both an individual and a family maximum out-of-pocket is because some plans require the family unit (2+ members) to reach individual deductible while others require two times the individual maximum out of pocket, before they will cover at 100%.

The plans that allow each individual to reach their own is called an embedded plan. Once the individual reaches their own maximum out-of-pocket, the insurance company will cover 100% of their future services for that year while the other family members may still be subject to co-pays, deductible, and coinsurance.

The coinsurance percent is due once you have met your deductible.

	BRONZE	SILVER	GOLD
Total Cost of Services Received:	$15,500	$15,500	$15,500
Less Deductible:	($6,500)	($4,250)	($1,500)
Ramining Amount Subject to the Coinsurance percent	$9,000	$11,250	$14,000

Here is the full calculation for in-network services received:

	BRONZE	SILVER	GOLD
Total Cost of Services Received:	$15,500	$15,500	$15,500
Less Deductible:	($6,500)	($4,250)	($1,500)
Amount Subject to Coinsurance	$9,000	$11,250	$14,000
Times Coinsurance	50%	30%	20%
Coinsurance Amount	$4,500	$3,375	$2,800
Plus Deductible	$6,500	$4,250	$1,500
Total Amount	$11,000	$7,625	$4,300
	Note: If this Total Amount is less than your deductible, you will pay that amount. If it is more, you will only pay the maximum out-of pocket		
Your Responsibility	$9,450	$7,625	$4,300
Keep in mind…	You would pay $9450 because it is the max out-of-pocket	You would pay $7625 because it is less than your $9100 max out-of-pocket	You would pay $4300 because it is less than your $7000 max out-of-pocket

PRIMARY CARE, SPECIALISTS, AND URGENT CARE

"I have a doctor that I want to see. He is my cardiologist. How much do I pay to visit him?"

This was a typical Tuesday morning question. Okay, it was typical any day, really.

Primary care provider visits should be your primary source of medical attention. The reasons are that your costs will usually be lower, and they are your point of contact for care and possible referrals.

	BRONZE	SILVER	GOLD
Primary Care (PCP)	$50 *	First 3 visits $5 *, then $45 *	$20 *
Specialist	$100 *	$65 *	$40 *
Urgent Care	$100	$65 *	$40 *

Indicates the deductible is waived

For Primary Care Physician office visits costs will depend on the plan and metal tier that you choose based on the number of visits and co-pay expense for each visit.

For example:

- Bronze plan will allow you to go to your primary care provider and specialist at a co-pay. It will not waive the deductible for urgent care, which means you need to pay the deductible amount before you begin to pay the flat co-pay amount.
- Silver plan allows the first three visits at a lower amount and once you get to the fourth visit, the co-pay amount goes up. This

plan has co-payment for specialists and urgent care.

- Gold plan has lower co-pays for primary care, specialist, and urgent care.

Prescription drugs

The importance of prescription drugs is that you would need to know what you need in any plan year. Think about what prescriptions you take regularly. Now, think about if it is a generic drug, a preferred brand name, a non-preferred brand name, or a specialty (those that you regularly see advertised).

Generic prescriptions have the same active ingredients as brand-name prescriptions (they may have different inactive ingredients). They become available after the patent expires on a brand name prescription and are 20-80% less.

Preferred Brand prescriptions have been on the market for some time, are widely known and accepted, but do not have a generic equivalent. They cost more than generics.

Non-Preferred Brand prescription is one that is not included in the insurance carrier's formulary or list of preferred drugs. They are usually newer to the market and have a preferred alternative drug.

They have higher co-insurance than preferred and generic prescriptions.

Specialty prescriptions usually require pre-authorization from the insurance carrier to be filled and sometimes are only available at specialty pharmacies. They require special handling, administration, and/or monitoring. These types of drugs usually are to treat complex, chronic, and/or costly conditions.

Once you know what you need and use, you will be able to determine how much you will spend each year on your prescriptions based on the plan that you choose.

	BRONZE	SILVER	GOLD
Generic	$20 *	$20 *	$10 *
Preferred Brand	no charge after ded	$65 *	$40 *
Non-Preferred Brand	no charge after ded	50% *	50% *
Preferred Specialty	no charge after ded	50% *	20% *
Non-Preferred Specialty	no charge after ded	50% *	50% *

*Indicates the deductible is waived

In this example, you will spend different amounts on the same prescription.

- The Bronze plan will allow you to purchase your Generic drugs at a flat dollar amount. For this plan, it is $20.

  All other prescription drugs are subject to the deductible before you pay the 50% co-insurance.

  Essentially, you will pay out-of-pocket for most of your prescriptions if they are not generic.

- Silver plan allows you to purchase your Generic and Preferred Brand Name drugs at a flat dollar amount, $20 and $65 respectively. Non-preferred drugs are at 50%.

  Specialty drugs are paid at 50% after the deductible has been reached.

- Gold plan allows you to purchase your Generic and Preferred Brand Name drugs at a flat dollar amount, $10 and $40 respectively. All other drugs are paid at a percent prior to reaching the deductible.

Keep in mind, if you have prescriptions that are a percent, you will be paying more than the flat dollar amount prescriptions. And, if your plan prescriptions are subject to the deductible, you will continue to pay even more.

ALL OTHER SERVICES

"What does my plan actually cover? When do I stop paying everything out of my pocket?"

Serious questions are made for clarification.

Without knowing how to use your plan or what your plan covers, you may become frustrated when you receive a bill in the mail weeks after getting labs or x-rays done.

Many plans will require that you pay the deductible before the insurance covers the costs of certain services.

There are some very rich plans that may provide services that are not subject to the deductible and some that may allow flat fees for services. Keep in mind, you may pay more monthly for those plans, but they may be worth it if you know you will be using those services.

	BRONZE	SILVER	GOLD
Inpatient care (including	50%	30%	20%
Outpatient x-rays & labs	50%	30%	20%
Emergency Room	50%	30%	20%
Alternative care	Not Covered	$40 *	$25 *

*Indicates the deductible is waived

Here is an example, of how you may pay more for the same service:

- Bronze plan requires you to reach your deductible before you pay 50% coinsurance for hospitalization, x-rays, laboratories, and emergency room.

  This means that you must have spent the first $6500 before you are able to pay 50% of the cost of the service.

- Silver plan requires you to reach your deductible before you pay 30% co-insurance for hospitalization, x-rays, laboratories, and emergency room.

  This particular Silver plan allows Alternative care visits to your chiropractor and acupuncturist at a co-pay.

  This plan requires you to spend the first $4,250 before you can pay 30% of the cost of the service.

- Gold plan requires you to reach your deductible before you pay 20% co-insurance for hospitalization, x-rays, laboratories, and emergency room.

  This particular Gold plan allows Alternative care visits to your chiropractor and acupuncturist at a co-pay.

  This plan requires you to spend the first $1,500 before you can pay 20% of the cost of the service.

5

HOW DO I PAY?

An explanation of benefits (EOB) is a statement sent by the insurance carrier to the member explaining the treatments and/or services were paid on their behalf or denied.

The EOB may identify:

The patient

The date of service

The provider

The service provided

The amount charged by the provider

The amount of the charges that are covered and not covered under your plan

The amount paid to your provider

The amount you are responsible for

You will notice that the EOB will state "This is Not a Bill." It simply gives you information to know what you may expect to have to pay out of pocket.

The provider may send you a bill before your insurance pays them; therefore, you may see a bill for the full amount. It is important that you wait for your EOB before paying the provider, as you may overpay.

Once the insurance carrier pays the provider, you will receive an updated bill from the provider with any charges that you are still responsible for.

Health Insurance Company

EXPLANATION OF BENEFITS
THIS IS NOT A BILL

Jane Smith
123 SW Main St
Anytown, OR 97205

Subscriber Information
Member ID: XYZ123456789
Group ID: 123456

Patient Name: Jane Smith
Place of Service: Outpatient
Date Received: 0101/2021

Claim Number: 01122334455Z
Type of Service: Medical
Date Processed: 02/01/2021

Provider: ER & Hospital
Payment to: ER & Hospital

| | | | | | Patient Responsibility | | | | |
Date of Service	Total Charges	Other Insurance	Amount Paid	Notes	Non-covered Charges	Deductible	Co-insurance	Co-pay	Total Patient Responsibility
01/01/2021	$$$	$$$	$$$		$$$	$$$	$$$	$$$	$$$
01/01/2021	$$$	$$$	$$$		$$$	$$$	$$$	$$$	$$$
Claim Total	$$$	$$$	$$$		$$$	$$$	$$$	$$$	$$$

Explanation of the EOB sections:

Benefit paid to provider: The total dollar amount paid to the provider for the services rendered.

Claim: The claim number generated by their system.

Comments: The explanation of listed codes and the information regarding your benefits.

Copay: The amount you owe on the remaining covered charges after your plan's benefits have been applied.

Deductible: Charges that have been applied to your plan's deductible. Any amounts listed in this column are your responsibility and subtracted from the remaining covered charges before any benefits are applied.

For services from to: The date the service was provided.

Non-covered charges: Amount (if any) that is a non-covered charge and being denied.

Patient: The name of the patient.

Patient responsibility: Amount you are responsible for paying your provider, which is the total of disallowed charges (charges not covered by your insurance carrier), charges applied to your deductible, and copayments.

Payee: The provider, subscriber, or healthcare location receiving payment.

Proc code: The procedure code number. This is not required and may not appear.

Provider: The name of provider (physician, nurse, physical therapist, practitioner, etc.) seen by the patient.

Provider discount/disallow: Amount you saved by using an in-network provider.

Remaining covered charges: Amount less any disallowed charges and charges that were applied to your deductible and provider discount. Your plan's benefits are applied towards the amount listed in this column.

Total benefit: The total amount the insurance carrier will pay for services.

Total charges: The amount charged for services.

Type of service: A description of the service performed.

What if things don't look right?

Always check your EOB (Explanation of Benefits) against the medical bill from the provider. In most cases, you will receive the medical bill prior to the EOB.

Once you receive the EOB, you will receive a   second bill from your provider with discounts and contracted amounts they will charge.

If dates, services, or amounts do not make sense to you, it is okay to question the provider and the insurance carrier.

If you have questions:

1 Make a phone call to your **PROVIDER** to ask.
2 Then, contact the insurance carrier to check the answer received by the provider.

You may need to call the provider back again to provide the information received and possibly have them correct the billing or coding.

Always obtain a reference number and name of who you speak with at the insurance carrier. Give that to the provider's billing department and ask them to call the insurance company when there is a discrepancy to have it corrected.

Be timely in calling!

Most insurance carriers can only go back 1 year to correct a discrepancy, even if it is in your favor.

6

PAINT ME A PICTURE

INDIVIDUAL TAX CREDIT SCENARIOS

Example #1

Family of four with income of $50,000

Income as a percentage of federal poverty level is at 224 percent. The children would likely qualify for Medicaid or Children's Health Insurance Program (CHIP).

For the parents, the Premium for a mid-level Silver plan: $927 per month

Advanced Premium Tax Credit (APTC): $781 per month

Qualify for Cost-Sharing reduction of deductible, maximum out-of-pocket, and co-payments.

Net Premium: $146 per month

Example #2

40-year-old individual with income of $30,000

Income as a percentage of federal poverty level: 250 percent

Premium for plan: $474 per month

Advanced Premium Tax Credit (APTC): $354 per month

Net Premium: $120 per month

Note: The advanced premium tax credits and premiums for these examples are hypothetical. Depending on your state, plans, rates, family composition, and household income, these numbers will change yearly. Be sure to update your income at least once a year during open enrollment.

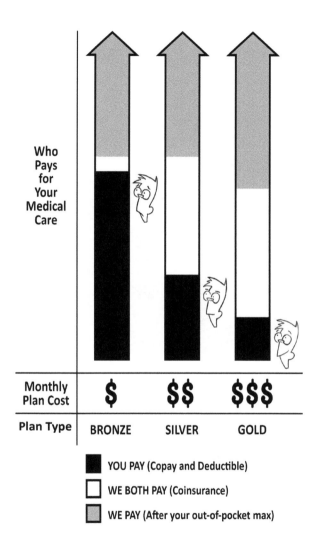

APPENDIX

Actual Rates - developed and presented to individuals or group applicants after they have provided specific demographic information.

Adjustment Type - deducted from income on Federal tax returns in order to arrive at your Modified Adjusted Gross Income (MAGI).

Advance premium tax credit (APTC) - Based on where the individual/family lives, their age(s), household composition, and income, it is the determination of what that individual or family should receive to reduce their health care insurance premium. If a person qualifies for advance payment of premium tax credits (APTC), the amount will be applied right away and sent directly to the insurance company each month to reduce the premium they pay. See also "APTC."

Affordable Care Act (ACA) - The Affordable Care Act (ACA) is the health care reform law enacted in March 2010 that mandates all Americans have health insurance coverage. It puts individuals, families, small businesses and Tribal organizations in control of selecting and managing their insurance coverage. It also provides other reforms, including guaranteed coverage regardless of an individual's health status.

Agent - licensed health insurance agents. They help individuals and small employers by guiding them through the complexities of purchasing and enrolling in health insurance coverage to get the best price based on specific situations and needs. Agents also act as advisors when clients need help navigating claims processing after they incur services. Agents are paid a commission for their work, which does not increase the cost of insurance coverage.

APTC - refers to advance payment of premium tax credits. If a person qualifies for APTC, the amount will be applied right away and sent directly to the insurance company each month to reduce the premium the individual pays to the insurance company.

Authorized Representative - a person, such as a guardian or an individual who has power of attorney, who is authorized to help make decisions for others. These decisions include enrolling in a health coverage plan or handling claims and payments. An authorized representative may sign the application on behalf of the enrollee.

Balance Billing - occurs when a provider bills the insured individual for the difference between the provider's charge and the allowed amount. A preferred provider may not balance bill for covered services.

Benefits - refer to any available services under health coverage.

Carrier - a licensed company that provides health and/or dental insurance coverage for individuals, families, and groups. A carrier may also be referred to as an 'insurer' or 'insurance company.'

Children's Health Insurance Program (CHIP) - provides health coverage for children whose families can't afford private insurance. CHIP is administered by each state and jointly funded by the federal and state governments.

COBRA - type of continuation coverage that allows employees and their families to temporarily continue their health coverage offered through an employer, even if they have changed or lost a job, or experienced a change in their eligibility status. Usually for up to 18 months.

Coinsurance - the insured individual's share of costs for a covered health care service. This is calculated as a percentage (e.g., 20 percent) of the allowed amount for the service before or after the deductible is met. The insurer pays the rest of the allowed amount.

Copayment (Copay) - is the fixed dollar amount (e.g., $25) an insured person pays for a covered health care service. Copayment amounts can change depending on the type of service received.

Cost Sharing - refers to any expense paid by an individual for essential health benefits such as deductibles, copayments, and coinsurance. These costs are above and beyond the amount the individual pays for a premium.

Cost-Sharing Reduction - lower the maximum out-of-pocket limits, and they reduce silver plan deductibles, co-pays, and coinsurance amounts for certain qualified applicants.

Deductible - is the amount an individual or family must pay for health care services before the insurer begins to pay for services. The deductible may not apply to all services.

Dependent - individuals and family members of the subscriber (other than the taxpayer or spouse) who qualify as an exemption on the subscriber's tax returns. Dependents are eligible to enroll for coverage on the subscriber's medical or dental plan.

Descendant of a Tribal Member - the offspring of an enrolled member of a federally recognized Tribe, up to two levels. For example, a descendant would be the offspring of a parent or grandparent who is/was an enrolled member of a federally recognized Tribe.

Durable Medical Equipment (DME) - supplies sometimes ordered by a health care provider for an individual's routine or extended use. Coverage for DME may include oxygen equipment, wheelchairs, crutches, or blood-testing strips for diabetics.

Eligible Dependent - individuals—spouse, domestic partner, or child—who are eligible to enroll in the same plan as the subscriber.

Employer Coverage - the health coverage that a company provides to its employees.

Essential Health Benefits (EHB) - a set of 10 health care service categories defined by the Affordable Care Act (ACA) that must be covered by certain plans beginning in 2014.

Exclusive Provider Organization (EPO) -plans that generally require use of in-network providers (like HMO plans) and may not cover out-of-network providers, except in emergencies. A person covered by an EPO plan generally does not have to choose a primary care physician (PCP) or get a referral to see a specialist, but they typically have a lower cost share when using providers who are in the EPO network.

Federal Poverty Level (FPL) - is the most recently published federal poverty level as of the first day of the annual open enrollment period for coverage in a quality health plan (QHP).

Federally Recognized Tribe - American Indian Tribes legally acknowledged by the United States Bureau of Indian Affairs. Federal Tribal recognition gives Tribes certain rights and benefits. There are currently 566 federally recognized Tribes.

Financial Help - refers to the help an individual may receive to help pay for coverage. Financial help includes premium tax credits, cost-sharing reductions, Medicaid, CHIP, and other public programs.

Formulary - refers to the list of drugs that is approves and prefers for certain medical conditions. It lists what drugs the insurance plan covers and at what level they are covered. Insurance companies negotiate the prices of drugs on their formularies with drug manufacturers.

Grievance - written complaints that insured people file with their health insurance carrier if they are unsatisfied or have a problem with their coverage.

Gross Income - total dollar amount a person receives as money, goods, property, and services. Gross income is not tax exempt.

Health Care Provider - doctors and other medical professionals who help identify, treat, and prevent illness or disability.

Health Insurance - an agreement by a carrier to pay some or all of an individual's health care costs, as long as the individual pays the monthly premium established under his or her plan.

Health Maintenance Organization (HMO) - plans that usually offer a wide range of health services within a limited network of providers. A person covered by an HMO may have to choose an in-network primary care physician (PCP) and may need a referral to see a specialist. Services that are provided by out-of-network providers or without a referral may not be covered or may have a much higher cost share.

Health Savings Account (HSA) - tax-sheltered savings accounts that beneficiaries covered by qualified high-deductible health plans can use to pay for health care expenses outside of their health plan. Money remaining in the account at the end of the year may be used the following year. Contributions to an individual's HSA can be made by anyone, including an employer, up to an annual maximum.

High-Deductible Health Plan (HDHP) - a health insurance plan with lower premiums and higher deductibles than a traditional health plan. Enrollment in an HDHP allows an insured person to sign up for a health savings account.

HIPPA - Health Insurance Portability and Accountability Act is a federal law that gives you rights over your health information and sets rules and limits on who can look at and receive your health information.

Household - includes a person, his or her spouse or live-in partner, any children who live with them, and anyone they include on his or her federal income tax return.

In-Network Benefits - associated with a health insurance carrier's network of doctors, hospitals, clinics, and labs that accept allowed amounts as payment in full. Patients typically pay lower out-of-pocket costs when they use these providers. Inpatient care - medical or surgical care that requires admission to a hospital or medical facility and usually includes an overnight stay.

Legally Present Resident - a person who is not a U.S. citizen and lives under legally recognized and lawfully recorded permanent residence as an immigrant.

Managed Care Organization (MCO) - networks or health plans are doctors, clinics, hospitals, pharmacies, and other providers who work together to care for their members' health care needs.

Marketplace - refers to a health insurance exchange, which the Affordable Care Act (ACA) requires each state to establish. Individuals and small employers can use the marketplace to compare plans and sometimes access financial assistance to help pay for health coverage. States may implement their own or opt for a federally facilitated marketplace.

Medicaid - federal and state program that helps with medical costs for people with limited income and resources and offers coverage for aging and disability programs.

Medically Necessary - health care services or supplies are those needed to prevent, diagnose, or treat an illness, injury, condition, disease, or its symptoms, and that meet accepted standards of medicine.

Metal Level - the four levels of health insurance coverage (bronze, silver, gold, and platinum) available to individuals and groups under the Affordable Care Act (ACA). Each metal level must cover the same set of minimum essential health benefits, and it may contain additional benefits. of all insurance plans available.

Network - facilities, providers and suppliers' contract with health insurance carriers or plans to provide health care services.

Non-Preferred Provider - doctors or other medical professionals who do not have a contract with an insured person's carrier or plan. People will usually pay more to see a non-preferred provider.

Open Enrollment - annual period that usually occurs shortly before the beginning of a new plan year, during when individuals, families, and employees may enroll in a private health insurance plan for the first time, make changes to an existing plan, switch carriers, or cancel their coverage.

Out-Of-Network Benefits - associated with non-contracted health care providers. Some plans offer out-of-network benefits, but people typically pay higher out-of-pocket costs for these services and may have to file a separate claim.

Out-Of-Pocket Costs - expenses for medical care that aren't covered or paid by an individual's or group's insurance plan, including deductibles, coinsurance, and copayments, plus all other costs for services that aren't covered.

Out-Of-Pocket Maximum (OOP Max) - the amount an insured person will have to pay in out-of-pocket costs within a policy period. Health insurance carriers will begin paying 100 percent of health care costs after the out-of-pocket limit has been reached. Each plan has limits and exclusions not included in the out-of-pocket limit.

Outpatient Care - medical or surgical care that does not include an overnight hospital stay.

Point Of Service (POS) Plan - a hybrid of HMO and PPO plans, in which the insured person chooses a primary care physician who refers patients to specialists. The insured person may also receive care from non-network providers, but with higher out-of-pocket costs.

Preferred Provider Organization (PPO) - allow the insured person to choose their own providers. A person covered by a PPO typically does not have to choose a primary care physician (PCP) or be referred to a specialist.

Premium - the amount that an insured person must pay for health coverage. It is usually paid monthly, quarterly, or yearly.

Prescription Drug Benefit - helps pay for prescription drugs and medications.

Prescription Drugs - require a prescription from medical professionals before they may be dispensed.

Preventive Care - consists of measures taken to prevent disease or injury.

Primary Care Provider - directly deliver or coordinate a range of health care services for their patients.

Private Health Insurance - coverage by a health plan provided through an employer or union or purchased by an individual from a private health insurance company.

Probationary Period - the time period determined by the employer— that employees must wait before becoming eligible for group benefits after their date of hire. Effective January 1, 2014, the Affordable Care Act (ACA) does not allow this period to be greater than 90 days.

Provider - any doctor or other medical professional, or a health care facility rendering services that are licensed, certified, or accredited as required by state law. This includes primary care physicians or providers, nurse practitioners, clinical nurse specialists, or physician assistants, as allowed under state law, who directly provide, coordinate, or help patients access a range of health care services. Preferred providers are doctors or other medical professionals who have a contract with a health insurance carrier to provide health care services.

Qualified Health Plan (QHP) - an insurance plan (certified by an exchange/marketplace) that provides essential health benefits and follows established limits on cost sharing (deductibles, copayments, and out-of-pocket maximum amounts).

Qualifying Event - after an open enrollment period ends, a qualifying event is required for most people to change their existing health plan or enroll in a plan for the first time. Certain life changes –

like marriage, moving, loss of health coverage, or birth or adoption of a child – could lead to a qualifying event. People who have a qualifying event and are eligible for health coverage will be able to enroll in or change plans during a special enrollment period.

Section 125 Premium-Only Plan (POP) - legally allows employees to pay their portion of medical insurance premiums and other benefit premiums using pre-tax or tax-free dollars.

Small Business Health Care Tax Credit - was created under the Affordable Care Act (ACA) to help encourage small businesses with fewer than 25 employees to offer group coverage to their employees. To receive the tax credit, small businesses must pay average annual wages of less than $50,000 per employee, pay at least 50 percent of the employee-only premiums (not dependent premiums) and purchase one or more certified medical and/or dental plans.

State Continuation - type of continuation of coverage that allows employees and their families to temporarily continue their health coverage offered through an employer, even if they have changed or lost a job, or experienced a change in their eligibility status. Usually for up to nine months and for employers with 20 or less employees.

Tax Credit - a sum deducted from the total amount taxpayers owe on their taxes. See also: 'Advanced Premium Tax Credit' or 'APTC.'

Tax-Filing Status - based on marital status and family situation. A taxpayer can fall into one of five filing status categories: single, married filing jointly, married filing separately, head of household, and a qualifying widow(er) with dependent children.

Urgent Care - medical care reserved for an illness, injury or condition serious enough that a person would seek care right away.

ABOUT THE AUTHOR

Gladys Monroy Boutwell comes with over 20 years of corporate America experience, including international business-to-business, in-depth writing of training material, and leadership roles.

She has an MBA in International Business and Leadership & Management from University of La Verne, is Six Sigma Green Belt Certified through Microsoft, was a Certified Payroll Professional while at ADP, is a John Maxwell Certified international coach and speaker, and is a *Madrina de Salud* award recipient.

As an insurance agent, she is licensed in health, life, property, and casualty. She has a Certified Insurance Counselor (CIC) Certification.

With the support of the Guatemalan President Otto Pérez Molina, Gladys was one of 150 John Maxwell coaches that conducted transformational leadership training for 22,000 citizens in 2013.

She was a contributing author in The Gratitude Project: Celebrating 365 Days of Gratitude 2013 Edition by Donna Kozik and Heart of a Toastmaster by Sheryl L. Roush. Additionally, she has contributed to Examiner.com, EcoBuzzLA.com, Guatemala Próspera, Productive Flourishing, BermudaBob.com, Pulse, BuildingWhatMatters.com, StarWorldWideNetworks.com, Comtivate Radio Network, "How to be a Speaker" tour, Toastmasters District 7, Toastmasters District 23, the TLN Show, Stand Up and Speak radio show, and Rough Notes magazine.

Gladys sees the importance of education of businesses in the need to protect their assets. She focuses on what is most important to the business owner and how she can share knowledge that will benefit that business.

She utilizes her Spanish-speaking skills to communicate and educate staff that prefer to obtain information in their native language.

To contact Gladys:

Insurance by Design

30150 SW Parkway Ave, Suite 200, Wilsonville, OR

503-433-7965 or 503-482-7050

gladys@insurancedesignpros.com

www.InsuranceDesignPros.com

SOURCES AND LINKS

Forbes' *Five Things You Need to Know Before Buying Health Insurance*

Forbes' *Medical Myth: All Health Insurance Plans Created Equal*

Link to "Find an Agent Database" at the *National Association of Benefits and Insurance Professionals* website: https://nabip.org/looking-for-an-agent/find-an-agent

Affordable Care Act Summary: http://obamacarefacts.com/

Health Insurance Marketplace calculator: https://www.kff.org/interactive/subsidy-calculator/

Health Plan and Savings Account Comparison chart: http://www.healthinsurance.info/guide/compare

Six of One – Obamacare vs. The Affordable Care Act: www.youtube.com/watch?v=sx2scvIFGjE

U.S. Treasury, Kaiser Family Foundation